The Fellowship of Angels

Richard Rolle

The Fellowship of Angels

The English Writings
of Richard Rolle

Translated into modern English
by Henrietta Hick

GRACEWING

First published in 2008

Gracewing
2 Southern Avenue
Leominster
Herefordshire HR6 0QF

ISBN 978 0 85244 123 7

Cover picture: *Richard the Hermit.* By permission of
The British Library STOWE.39 f 16v

Frontispiece: *Richard Rolle.* By permission of
The British Library COTTON.FAUSTINA.B.VI f 186

Typeset by Action Publishing Technology Ltd,
Gloucester GL1 5SR

Contents

Acknowledgements

This translation of a selection of writings of Richard Rolle from Middle English began after seeing references to him in guide books when first coming to Pickering. The librarians, to whom my thanks are due, aquired for me the collections of Carl Horstmann, H. E. Allen and F. M. Comper, and it seemed to me that some might enjoy to read his life and works in more modern English.

I wish to express my grateful thanks for the help and expertise of Lucy Beckett, the encouragement of Canon Francis Hewitt, Fr Keith Hutchinson and John Dean and to John Rushton for useful historical information, to Judy Dixon who aided an initial leaflet, my 'secretarial team': daughter Jeany Robinson, granddaughter Emily Hick, and 'Tasia Scrutton, who also checked the presentation and provided some photographs as did Ian Riley, and to John Jennison for the fine drawing of Pickering Church. Thanks too to Sharon Hepton for some final typing.

I am also indebted to Anthony Musson for obtaining the Cotton portrait of R. Rolle, Hermit, and, organising and composing music 'Sweet Jesu, now will I sing' for the concert given in SS Peter and Paul, Pickering in honour of Richard, and for his encouragement.

To all these my thanks are due, and to any I may have missed, my sincere apologies.

Illustrations

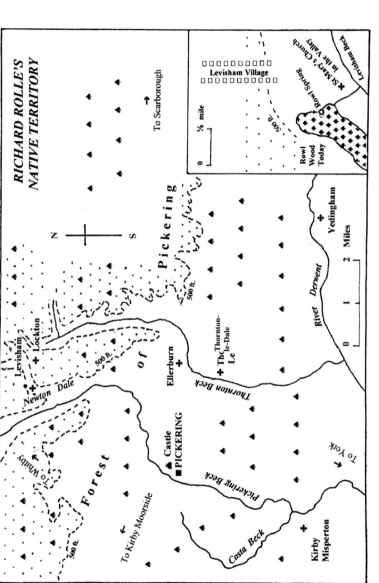

1. Richard Rolle's native territory

2. St Hilda's Ellerburn, Thornton-le-Dale – exterior

3. St Hilda's Ellerburn, Thornton-le-Dale – interior

4. Viking stone carving from St Hilda's Ellerburn,
Thornton-le-Dale

5. Richard Rolle's gravestone, Hampole Priory

6. Pickering Church today

Introduction

Richard Rolle, ardent medieval spiritual writer, eloquent religious guide, fervent hearer of the song of angels, was, according to C. Horstman,[1] the true Father of English literature. His great body of writing included lyrics, commentaries and treatises in Latin and English, letters and devotional works, and translations from Latin. His works were much loved and widely read until the Reformation; some were printed by Wynkyn de Worde, and many manuscript copies of his works exist.

Richard was born c.1300 at 'Thornton near Pickering'. There are a number of Thorntons in Yorkshire, but Thornton-le-Dale is thought to be the most likely; it is also thought that his father was engaged in work connected with Pickering Forest, a Royal hunting ground. His parents sent him to school and, in his mid-teens, he was maintained at Oxford University by Thomas Neville who was the son of Lord Raby. Neville later became Archdeacon of Durham Cathedral. It is possible that Richard was a member of Balliol College which had been founded by John de Balliol (father of King John de Balliol of Scotland) and his widow Dervorguilla around 1282, as the result of a penance imposed on Balliol by the Bishop of Durham. Richard was a good student and considered 'how he could

---

[1.] Horstman, C., *Richard Rolle of Hampole and his Followers*, London, 2 Vols, 1895.

best serve God and avoid the share of worldly temptation'. When Richard went up to Oxford it had been a
centre of learning for about a hundred years. The religious
houses produced many excellent teachers, and from 1214,
Chancellors were appointed, representing the Bishop of
Lincoln. One of the first was Robert Grosseteste[2] who
taught the Franciscans. He insisted that the first lecture of
the day should be on Sacred Scripture. There were many
eminent philosophers among the Franciscans in the thir-
teenth and fourteenth centuries, including Duns Scotus,[3]
Roger Bacon and William of Ockham,[4] although great
learning was not at all what St Francis intended when he
founded his Order!

Perhaps something of this was in Richard's mind when
he returned home in his twentieth year, determined to be
a hermit. He said to his sister, 'Dear Sister, you have two
kirtles, one white and one grey which I need, please bring
them to me in the wood tomorrow together with Father's
rain-hood.'

Wondering what was in his mind, she agreed and
brought them to him; telling her to turn her back, he cut
the sleeves from the grey kirtle, put the white one on and
the grey over the top and, with the rain-hood, felt he had
improvised a suitable hermit's habit. When he called on
his sister to look, she was horrified and ran home shout-
ing, 'My brother is mad.' Richard made off into the woods
before any of his family could stop him.

Possibly Richard thought he would make a hut to live in
from the fallen branches, as no doubt he had done with his
friends in his childhood. About four miles away, near St
Mary's Church between Lockton and Levisham there is a

[2.] Robert Grosseteste (1175–1253): polymath, Bishop of Lincoln and
Chancellor of the University of Oxford.

[3.] Johannes Duns Scotus (c.1265–1308): Scottish philosopher and Franciscan. Taught at Oxford and Paris.

[4.] William of Ockham (c.1270–1349): English philosopher Franciscan
and original thinker. Deviser of Ockham's razor: 'It is in vain to do
with more what can be done with fewer.'

Rowl Wood, and Rowl Spring, thought to be associated with him. This in summer would be a delightful place to start on a solitary life, with the song of the birds to wake him for his prayers, and the sweet scent of the wild flowers for incense. There would be trout in the beck and in July he may have gathered wild raspberries; very likely curious neighbours came to look at him, perhaps sending their children to take him food from their tables.

The next time we hear of Richard, it is on the eve of the feast of the Assumption, 14 August. Richard is in church, probably SS Peter and Paul, Pickering, standing in the place where Lady de Dalton, the wife of John de Dalton (Constable of the Castle, Steward of the Manor, Keeper of the Forest for the Earl of Lancaster) used to pray. She would not allow anyone to disturb him and, it seems, was much taken by this devout youth. After Vespers her sons told her that he was Richard Rolle with whom they had been at Oxford, and the son of William Rolle, an old friend of their father.

The next day, on the feast of the Assumption of Our Lady, Richard sang at Matins, and afterwards served the priest at Mass. When the Gospel had been read he asked the priest's blessing, and climbing up into the pulpit, preached so beautifully that many in the congregation were moved to tears and said he was a 'special instrument of the Holy Ghost'.

After Mass, John de Dalton invited Richard to dinner with his family, but when he entered the manor, he felt so shy that he tried to hide in a disused room, perhaps afraid that he would be sent back to his father. However, Dalton sought him out, and brought him to the table, and set him 'above his own sons'. Richard ate in silence, and tried to leave as soon as possible, but Dalton prevailed on him to stay, as he wished to have some words with him in private. He asked him if he were the son of his old friend William Rolle, and when Richard admitted as much, he talked to him about his aims, and being convinced of his sincerity and the 'sanctity of his purpose', fitted him out with clothes more suitable for a hermit, and gave him a room for a cell, and supplied him with food and drink.

It is possible that Richard had received Minor Orders before he left Oxford. Opinions vary as to whether he was ordained priest at some later date; there is no evidence to prove it except that he appears to have had further study, he addressed books on spiritual direction to priests and, himself became a spiritual director towards the end of his life. Meanwhile, with the Daltons, he prayed, meditated, studied and sought to advance in spiritual life; here he wrote *Canticum Amoris* and *Judica Me* and here, as he tells us in *Incendium Amoris* (written towards the end of his life) he had his first mystical experience. It was 'three years, less three or four months', from the time of his conversion until 'the day when the door of Heaven swung back and his Face was revealed, so that my inner eye could contemplate the things that are above and see by what way it might find the Beloved and cling to him ...'[5]

He goes on to say that while sitting in a chapel, delighting in the sweetness of meditation, he felt an incredibly delightful warmth. In the same chapel nine months later, whilst saying the night psalms, he experienced the divine presence more deeply, which he describes as becoming aware of 'a symphony of song, and in myself ... a corresponding harmony, at once wholly delectable and heavenly, which persisted in my mind ... my thinking turned itself into melodious song, and my meditation became a poem and my very prayers and psalms took on the same sound'.[6] Richard had a great love and devotion to the Holy Name of Jesus; he would pray and meditate, and look forward to dying surrounded by angelic harmony.

Richard had prepared himself to receive these gifts (which he acknowledged were not for any merit on his part), by leading an austere life, by spurning the world, and its vanities, by 'fixing his mind on Heaven and desir-

[5] Wolters, Clifton (trans.), *The Fire of Love*.
[6] Wolters, Clifton (trans.), *The Fire of Love*.

ing to depart and be with Christ his most Sweet Beloved'.[7]

It is written of him that many were converted to God by his exhortations, writings, treatises, and little books which he composed for his neighbours and which sounded like 'the sweetest music'. As is not uncommon with holy men, strange stories are told of him. He was speaking with some ladies one afternoon, while writing at the same time, and the spoken word was said to be different from the written. Once he was so absorbed in his meditation that he was quite unaware when the cloak he was wearing was taken from him, patched and replaced upon him.

The ladies seem to have been fond of him. Those who disapproved of a freelance hermit not subject to the discipline of a Religious Order complained that he laughed and chattered with girls. He criticised the Clergy and Religious and some spoke ill of him, though gradually he mellowed and modified his outspoken ways.

Dalton's appointment in Pickering ended in 1322 (after Thomas Earl of Lancaster was executed following his rebellion against Edward II). In 1324 Roger de Kirkby conveyed to Dalton the manor of Kirkby Misperton. Richard moved on and his life was at times very hard; he sometimes lacked food and water, believing this sacrifice was in accordance with the Gospel: 'Because for the sake of his Saviour the hermit has made solitude his home, in Heaven he will receive a dwelling, golden and glistening in the midst of angelic orders. Because for the sake of his Creator he dressed in filthy rags, his maker will clothe him in eternal splendour.'[8]

At this time, Richard speaks of calumny and oppression on the part of those who had been his friends. Perhaps his patron was disappointed that this young man who had shown great promise should have left Oxford without an MA and become a wandering hermit, or giro-vagus,

[7.] Comper, F. M. (trans.), *Life and Lyrics of Richard Rolle.*
[8.] Wolters, Clifton (trans.), *The Fire of Love.*

generally regarded as a vagabond, rather like the New Age Travellers of today, or like the perpetual pilgrims of Holy Russia who were revered by some, by others regarded as idle layabouts.

Richard was not as far as we know attached to any religious order, but loved to meditate on Scripture. In the *Fire of Love* he quotes extensively from the Gospels, the Psalms, the Books of Wisdom and the Epistles of St Paul as well as the prophets, and in his love of Christ hears angelic song. He shows some affinity with Augustine of Hippo, since both sing God's praises with all the ardent fervour of a mystic and poet, yet find church music a distraction.

Not everyone then or later approved of his style of spirituality; the author of *The Cloud of Unknowing* says: 'The sound, gladness and sweetness that come from outside suddenly, – hold all these suspect.'[9] However, suspicion of even the greatest new ideas is hardly unprecedented: Robert Boenig says that around the same time the music of Guillaume de Machaut and Phillipe de Vitry's *Ars Nova* which broke new ground, moving away from the mathematical plainsong, and developing the polyphonic music 'whose aim was to delight the ear, sometimes at the expense of the words' met with the same kind of disapproval.[10]

In spite of the warnings of St John of the Cross against unbridled emotion, some people, yearning for the love of God, and in their awareness of the gift of his presence, are overcome by warmth, sweetness and delight. So St Thérèse of Lisieux feels love as a dart of fire. St Serafim of Sarov says 'God is fire, he warms the heart of our inner being.' Irina Ratushinskaia in her cold prison cell in the

---

9. Walsh, James (trans.), *The Cloud of Unknowing*, anon., New York, Paulist Press, 1981.
10. Boening, Richard, St Augustine's "Jubilus" and Richard Rolle's "Cantor", in *Vox Mystica*, Anne Clark Bartlett (ed.), Cambridge, 1995.

old Soviet Union would feel warmth and love and knew she was being prayed for.

Richard, during the time of his wandering, longed for a peaceful haven, feeling he was an outcast like Cain. He longed for some soul mate to sit with him and contemplate in silence 'and yearn after the joys of Eternal Love'. Then he remembered SS Cuthbert and Maglorius and Samson, who would sometimes leave abbey or diocese for a hermit's cell.[11] He exclaims, 'Celestial music resounds among them, and sweet flowing melody rejoices the solitary.'[12]

When Richard was offered hospitality in the houses of the rich he seems to have made himself very agreeable to the young people, while talking to them of faith, and of love of God. At times he seemed wary and apprehensive, since he was criticised for levity and familiarity with women, and it was suggested that when he sat meditating in the chapel, he was only sleeping off a good dinner! Later respect and affection were given to him, and he became more confident and less defensive. He never swerved from his awareness of Jesus as 'music at the feast, sweeter to the taste than honey and the honey-comb'.[13] Richard's writings, both prose and verse, are so full of poetry and joyfulness, that it is no wonder he became very popular, and many stories were told of wonderful answers to prayer. There was the lady, who on her deathbed was troubled by horrible demons who would not leave in spite of the prayers of her attendants. When Richard came to help her with his prayers, the demons fled. Where they had been, the rushes were burnt, and hoof prints seen in the ashes! He himself was once

11. Webb, J. F. (trans.), The Ven. Bede, *Life of St. Cuthbert*, London, Penguin, 1965. St Cuthbert: became Bishop of Hexham in 684, died a hermit on Farne in 687. His shrine is in Durham Cathedral. St Maglorius: sixth-century Welsh missionary and abbot. Companion of St Samson.
12. Wolters, Clifton (trans.), *The Fire of Love*.
13. Ecclesiasticus 49.1. (Old Testament 'Wisdom' book by Ben Sira *c.* 190 BC, written in Hebrew, translated into Greek by his grandson.)

tempted by a beautiful lady who held him so tight he was unable to move, but, calling on the Holy Name, he was able to touch the cross on his breast and the diabolical apparition, for such it was, vanished.

Around the middle of his life, Richard was living in Richmondshire, and later moved to Hampole, where he led a 'solitary life' and was spiritual director to the convent of Cistercian nuns. After he had died, the nuns, hoping for his early canonisation, prepared a biography in the form of lessons to be read during the Offices on his projected Feast Day. They also collected an account of the miracles that had been reported due to his intercession after his death.[14] The set of incidents that led to one such miracle, performed after Richard's death, began during his life, in the context of his friendship with the Lady Margaret Kirkby who had once been a recluse at Anderby. She was taken ill on 'The Day of the Lord's Supper' (Maundy Thursday). She was unable to speak and was in terrible pain. A 'Yeoman' of the town, knowing Richard had been instructing her 'in the art of loving God, and how to order her life' rode about twelve miles to ask him to come and help her.

Arriving with all speed, he found her still speechless and in pain, but after they had eaten together she fell asleep, lightly leaning against him, from which she awoke with such violent convulsions it seemed she would break the window, but she regained her speech with the words 'Glory to thee O Lord' and Richard answered 'Who is born of the Virgin' from the Compline hymn. The same thing happened again, when sitting in the same window. Margaret was seized by violent fits. Richard tried to hold her in safety, but she slipped though his hands and falling, awoke.

Richard said he thought he could have held on to her even had she been the Devil, but promised she would not

14. The York Breviary, Surtees Society. Vol. II, Appendix 5. 1882. This is the source of the unascribed biographical details and quotations.

suffer the same affliction again in his lifetime. Some years later Margaret again was ill, but without losing the power of speech, so she sent the Yeoman again to Hampole to see what had happened to Richard, as she knew he would faithfully keep his promise that she would not suffer again while he was alive. It was found that he had died shortly before her illness returned. Afterwards Margaret moved to Hampole where the body of Richard was buried; miraculously she never suffered from this illness again.

Richard's last years at Hampole seem to have been happy and he had a wide circle of affectionate admirers. He is said to have died of the Black Death at Michaelmas 1349. It would be a happy beginning to his seven-hundredth anniversary and the start of the new millennium if we could take a fresh look at his work, and accord it and him the recognition it deserves.

'With a song of joy come into my soul.
Show me something of your sweetness and charm when you so please!'

Writings of Richard Rolle

On Morning Prayer, on Rising

When you have gathered your wits together in your mind, and forgone those things that might hinder your prayer, and won to the devotion that God sends you through his most loving grace, quickly rise from your bed at the bell ringing, and if there be no bell, let the cock be your bell, and if there be neither cock nor bell, let God's love awaken you, for that most pleases him! And Jealousy, in love rises, awakens before both cock and bell, and has washed her face with sweet love-tears; and her soul within has joy in God with devotion and delight, yearning for him, and with heavenly happiness that God sends to those who Love him.

Most blessed are they whom love awakens, for they have many joys when others are fast asleep, and they find before them, what gladdens all, for God himself says this *'Qui mane vigilaverint ad me invenient me'* ('He that early awakens to me, he shall find me; to talk with him, to be happy with him and hear him.') Awake then, rise quickly and heartily thank your Lord God for the rest you had, and the watching of angels!

As a knight is full of joy at being called to come and speak with the king when he knows it is to his great profit, so with greater discernment, God's knight, that is, each Christian man, ought to be ready when his lord calls him for his great work.

Rise soberly with a glad heart, and think you hear God calling you with these words; 'Rise my love my fair one and show me your face, I yearn for the sound of your prayers ringing in my ears!'

Think when you rise how many perished, some burnt, some drowned, some died suddenly without repentance or shrift, their souls drawn to Hell by fiends, and some fallen into deadly sin, and from all of these perils God has delivered you of his goodness, and not for your desert! What have you done for God that he should shield you so? If you look well at what God does for you though you have not deserved it, you may find that God is always busy to work for you as if he had nothing else to do and forgotten all the world, and only thought of you!

When you have thus thought, lift up your heart to God and say 'I thank you dearest God with all my heart that have thus protected me this night, and sustained me with life and health, so keep me this day. Thank you lord for this great good and many others that you have done to me an unkind unworthy wretch, in spite of my evil deeds!' And put your self and all your friends in God's hands and say thus: 'Into your loving hands my Lord I yield my soul and my body and all my friends, brothers and sisters, and all that have done good to me in body or soul, and all Christian folk, for the love of your Mother, that beloved maiden, and the prayers of all your saints. Keep me this day (this night) from all perils of body or soul, and from all deadly sin, from all snares of the fiend, and sudden death and from the pains of Hell, and make us them to dread. Make our hearts holy with the grace of your Holy Spirit, so that whatever we do, we do your will, and never separate ourselves from you dear Lord. Amen.'

When you have done this, wend your way to the Kirk or Oratory, but if you may not reach one, make your chamber your Kirk! In the Kirk there is more devotion for prayer, for there is God on the Altar to hear those that pray to him, and grant them what they ask, or better, and being in the presence of the saints and the worship of the Kirk they are hallowed. Think of the angels that are there to serve their Lord and you, for their office is to receive your prayer and bear it to God, and bring you grace from him, as St Bernard says: 'Rise then quickly at God's call, and put from you all evil and answer your Lord with the words that Samuel said to God that called him: "Speak Lord, thy servant heareth".'

A Prayer

Jesu Criste, haue merci on me
As thou erte Kynge of Mageste,
And forgiffe me mi sinnes alle
That I haue donne bathe grette and smalle.
And brynge me if it be thi wille,
Til heuene to wonne with thee styl.

Spiritual Happiness

Spiritual happiness in Jesus and joyfulness of heart with sweetness in the soul, in the perfume of Heaven and in hopefulness, is health and healing.

My life dwells in Love, and lightsomeness frees my thoughts. I dread nothing that may work me woe, so much I know of well-being. It would be no wonder if death were dear to me, so that I might see him whom I seek, but now it is far from me, and I need to live here until he will release me.

Listen, and learn of his love, and you will not mistake it! Love makes me talk, and joy makes me chatter! See you live your life in light heartedness! Heaviness hold it away! Let not sadness sit with you, but rejoicing in God, ever-more make high glee!

Mirth in the Love of God

Laughter that comes of a happy conscience, and spiritual mirth, is to be praised, it is only found in the righteous, and it is called 'Mirth in the Love of God'.

Prayer to the Guardian Angels

O good and courteous Angel, ordained to be my Governor, I know well my feebleness and my foolishness, also well I know that strength have I none to do God's service, but only of his gift, and of your careful keeping. The knowledge that I have comes not from me, but what God will send me by your good entreaty. Now gracious Angel, I humbly ask you mercy, for little heed have I taken of your good advice; but now I thank you as well as I can with a full heart, that you may keep me truly this day and evermore, sleeping and waking with such defending and your holy teaching! Defend me and keep me from bodily harm, defend me and keep me from spiritual perils, for God's worship and the saving of my soul.

Teach me to know and understand how to worship and please God. Feed me with devotion and perfume of spiritual sweetness. Comfort me when in need against my spiritual enemies, and suffer me not to lose that grace that is granted me, but according to your worthy office, keep me in God's service to my life's end. And after the passing of the body, present my soul unto the merciful God. For though I fall all day by my own frailty, I take you to witness that ever I hope for mercy. Gladly would I worship God to your liking if I might, and after his holy teaching, and you also in him,

Thanks be to God. Amen.

To Young Maidens

Lo Christ, most lovely of all the sons of men, this King of Heaven desires your beauty, woos your love. He loves young maidens chaste and poor. He will adorn you with a wonderful crown, a worthy diadem, with shining garments, and she that now languishes for him in love, he will requite with everlasting sweetness.

The Fire of Love

Whilst I sat in a chapel at my prayers,
A Heavenly sound to me drew near,
For the Song of Songs first came to me
And my thought turned to love, speaking
Of the Heavenly and sweet harmony,
The which I took in mind delightfully.

Meditation on the Passion

(attribution to Rolle not certain)

For anguish of the pain that he would suffer, the blood dropped to the earth as sweat does in men in hard labour; and then St Michael came from his Father and said 'Lord Jesu, I and all the fair fellowship of angels have offered your sweat of blood to your Father and prayed for you', and he said 'My Son Jesus knows well that Man's soul needs to be bought with shedding of blood, and if he wills the health of Man's soul that we have always loved tenderly, he needs to die.'

Then this dear Lord answered and said these words of great love, 'The health of Man's soul, I will it always, so I shall choose to die so that Man's soul may be saved, rather than choose to escape death, and Man's soul perish; therefore not my will but my Father's be done.' Then Michael comforted Our Lord and said 'Be of good comfort dear Lord Jesus for it falls to him who is great to suffer great things, but soon the great suffering will be over, and afterwards shall come joy without end.'

Lord thy sorrows! Why were they not my death? Now they lead you forth naked, the tormentors and armed knights about you. The people pressed against you, they pushed and harried you shamefully, they spurned you with their feet as though you had been a dog. I see in my soul how pitifully you go, your body so bloody, so raw and blistered; your crown is so sharp that sits on your head; your hair moving in the wind, clotted with your blood; your lovely face so wan and swollen with buffeting and with beating, with spitting and spewing; your blood runs so, it makes me shudder to see, so horrifying they have made you seem, more like a leper than a clean man. The Cross is so heavy, so long, so rough, that they hung on your bare back, tied so tight!

Lady mercy! Why were you so bold among so many violent fools to follow so close? How was it that awareness of womanly or maidenly modesty had not kept you back? For it was not seemly for you to follow such a rabble, so vile and so shameful, so grisly to see! Lady, that sorrow that you suffered for your Son's Passion, that should have been mine, for I had deserved it and worse; I was the cause of it and he guiltless, so get me in your mercy a prick at my heart of that same pain, a drop of that sorrow to follow him with. If all that woe is mine by right, get me of my own, nor be so unjust as to withhold all! I do not ask for castles or towers nor other worldly wealth, the sun nor the moon nor the bright stars, but wounds of sorrow is all my desire, and compassion for my Lord Jesus Christ! I beseech my Lord for a drop of his red blood for my soul to wash it with!

I Sleep and My Heart Wakes

You that long for love, listen and hear of Love! In *The Song of Love* (Song of Solomon 5:2) it is written 'I Sleep and my heart wakes!' Much love he shows that never tires of loving, but always, standing, sitting, moving, or working, has love in his thoughts and in his dreams.

For the love I bear you, would that I might be that messenger that brings you to your Lord, that has made you and bought you, Christ the King, son of Heaven! For he will live with you if you will love him, and he asks no more but your love! And my dear sister in Christ, it is my will that you love him! Christ covets nothing but that you do his will, and leave all earthly love and desires that let you lose the true love of Jesus Christ. For while your heart is fastened to any bodily thing, you may not perfectly be united with God.

In Heaven are nine Orders of Angels that are contained in the Hierarchies. The lowest Hierarchy contains Angels, Archangels and Virtues. The middle Hierarchy contains Principalities, Powers and Dominions. The highest Hierarchy nearest God contains Thrones, Cherubim, and Seraphim. That Order which is least bright, is brighter than the sun is, as you see the sun is brighter than a candle, the candle brighter than the moon, the moon brighter than a star. So are the Orders in Heaven, each one brighter than the other from Angels to Seraphim. I say this to kindle your heart to long for the company of Angels.

For all that are good and holy, when they pass out of this world, shall be taken into these Orders, some into the lowest that have loved much, some into the middlemost that have loved more, others into the highest that have most loved God, and most burning in his love, as the Seraphim are. To which they are received that covet least in this world, and most sweetness feel in God, and whose heart is most burning in his love!

To you I write this specially, for I hope for more goodness in you than any other, and that you will give your thoughts to receive at death that which you see is most profitable for your soul, and that you may offer your heart to Jesus Christ, and leave the business of this world. For if you hold fast in burning love whilst you live here, without doubt your seat is ordained full high in Heaven, and joyful before God's face among his Holy Angels!

The Commandment to Love God

If you would find him, seek him inwardly in truth and hope, and the love of Holy Church, casting out all sin, and hating it in your heart, for that keeps him away from you, so that you may not find him.

The Shepherds that sought him found him lying in a crib between two beasts, as you know. If you truly seek him, you must go in the path of poverty, and not of riches. The star led the Three Kings to Bethlehem; there they found Christ swaddled in clouts, simply as a poor bairn! Thereby you understand that seeking him in pride and vanity will not find him.

A thing that I advise; do not forget this name 'Jesu' but think it in your heart night and day, as your special dear treasure! Love it more than your life, root it in your mind. Love Jesu for he made you and bought you full dearly. Give your heart to him for it is his due! Therefore set your love on his name Jesu. No evil thing may dwell in the heart where Jesu is truly held in mind for it chases away devils, destroys temptations, puts away any wicked deeds and vices, and cleanses thoughts. Who so loves it truly is full of God's grace and virtues; in spiritual comfort in this life, and when they die, they are taken up into the Orders of Angels, to see in endless joy Him whom they have loved! Amen

Written for a nun of Hampole

The Form of Perfect Living

To Margaret Kirkby, once recluse at Anderby

The Devil is the enemy of all Mankind, when he sees a man or a woman among a thousand turn wholly to God, and forsake all the vanities and riches that men that love this world covet, and seek lasting joy, he has a thousand wiles to try in what manner he may bring them into disarray. And when he cannot bring them to such sins that might make all men that knew them, wonder at them, he beguiles many so secretly, that often afterwards they do not know how they have been trapped.

Some he takes with the error he leads them into; some with conceit when he makes them think that the thing they say is the best, therefore they will take no advice from one who knows more than they do, and this is foul stinking pride, to set their wit above all other! Some the Devil deceives though vain-glory, that is idle joy. When they have pride and joy for the penance they suffer, or good deeds that they do or any virtue that they have, or are glad when men lack them, or are envious when others are highly praised, they hold themselves so glorious and so far passing the lives that other men lead, that they think that none should reproach them for anything they do or say, they despise them sinfully, none may bid them! How may you find a more sinful wretch? He is the worse that he is unaware, and is honoured by men as wise and holy.

Some are beguiled into too much liking for food and drink; some are deceived over too much abstinence of meat and drink and sleep, becoming so feeble that we may neither work nor pray as we should do, nor think! Are we not greatly to blame, that fail when we have most need to be stalwart?

If you would stand well with God, and have his grace rule in your life, and come to the joy of love, hold this name 'Jesus' so fast in you heart, that it can never leave your heart, and when you speak to your heart it says 'Jesus' through habit, and it shall be joy in your ear, honey in your mouth and music in your heart. For you shall rejoice to hear that name named, sweetness to speak it, mirth and song to think it.

If you think 'Jesus' continually and hold it fast, it purges your sin, and kindles the heart, and clears the soul, it removes anger and does away with sloth. It wounds with love and fills the soul with charity. It chases away the Devil, and puts away dread. It opens Heaven and makes a man contemplative. Have 'Jesus' in your mind, for it casts out all vices and phantoms. And hail Mary also both day and night, much love and joy you will feel if you keep this law. You need not study a great many books, hold love in your heart and in your work, and you will have all that we may say or write! For the fullness of the law is charity and in that hangs all.

Now Margaret, I have just said how you may come to perfection and to love him to whom you have taken yourself. If it does you good and helps you, thank God and pray for me! The grace of Jesus Christ be with you and keep you.

The Metrical Psalms

Richard Rolle made the first post-Norman-Conquest translation of the Psalms, starting with a metrical version, preserved in three northern manuscripts.[15]

Psalm 13

To when Lauerd forgetes thou me in ende?
Houlange saltou thi face fra me wende?
Houlange redes in mi saule set?
Sorwe in mi hert bi dai forthi?
To when sal mi fa houen ower me be?
Bihalde Lauerd mi God and here me.
Light min eghen and be mi rede,
Ne euer that I slepe in dede;
Leswhen mi withersin he say
'I betred againes him ai'
that droue me sal glade ife stired be I;
I soethli hoped in thi mercy.
Glade sal mi hert in hele thine,
I sal sing to Lauerd myne
That godes gave to me with blisse,
And salme to name ofe lauerd heghist isse.

15. Vesp. D. vii Egerton 614 Harl. 1770 MS belonged to the Abbey of Kirkham, near Malton.

Psalm 23

Lauerd me steres, noght wante sal me;
In stede of fode, there me louked he
He fed me ower watre ofe fode,
He led me ower sties of rightwisenes
For his name swa holi es.
For and ife I ga in mid schadw ofe dede
For thou with me erte iuil sal I noght drede
Thou yherde and thi stafe ofe mighte
Thai ere me roned dai and nighte
Thou graithe in mi sighte borde to be,
Againes thas that droued me,
Thou fatted in oli mi heued yhite
And me drinke dronken and while schire es ite!
And filigh me sal thi mercy
Alle daies of mi life forthi,
And that I wone in haus ofe Lauerd isse
In lengthe ofe daies al with blisse.

The Psalter

Richard Rolle is acclaimed as the first to translate the Psalms into English since the Conquest. The prose version followed the metrical version attributed to him, but used fewer older words.[16]

Prologue to the Psalter

(prose version)

Great abundance of spiritual comfort and joy comes to the hearts of those that say or sing the Psalms devoutly, loving Jesus Christ! They drop sweetness into men's souls and delight into their thoughts, and kindle their wills with the fire of love, making them hot and burning within, and fair and lovely in Christ's eyes. Those that last in their devotion, he raises to contemplative life, and often to the sound and mirth of Heaven.

The singing of psalms chases away fiends, brings angels to our help, it does away with sin, it pleases God, it fosters perfection. It banishes irritation and anger, and makes peace between body and soul. It brings desire of Heaven and contempt of earthly things. Truly this shining book is a chosen song before God, as a lamp lighting our life, health to a sick heart, honey to a bitter soul, dignity to spir-

16. Vesp. D. vii, Egerton 614 , Harl. 1770 MS belonged to the Abbey of Kirkham, near Malton.

itual people, speaking of secret virtues, which bring the
proud to meekness, and make kings subject to poor men,
fostering children with homeliness!

In them is so much beauty of understanding, and salu-
tary healing, that this book is called *A Garden Enclosed,
Wealth Secured, Paradise full of Apples*. Now with whole-
some teaching it brings troubled and stormy souls to a
peaceful life. Now admonishing to forgo sin with tears,
now promising joy to righteous men, now threatening
Hell to the wicked!

The song that delights the heart, and teaches the soul
joins with the singing of angels (whom we may not hear),
words of loving; so that he may think himself a stranger to
real life whoever has not the delightfulness of this gift of
wonderful sweetness, which does not sour through the
corruption of the world, but is everlasting in dignity, and
increasing in pure grace. All happiness and delight of
earth vanishes away, and at the last withers to nothing,
but this, the longer time it has, the more it is, and the most
of all at a man's death, when love is perfected!

This book is called the Psalter, named after a musical
instrument that in Hebrew is *Nablum*, in Greek *Psaltery*, in
English to 'Touch'. It has ten strings and a sound box, and
is played by the touching of the hand. Also this book
teaches us to keep the Ten Commandments, and not to
work for earthly things, but for Heaven which is above.

As this book is divided into thrice fifty psalms, so the
three states of Christian Man's religion are signified; the
first in penance, the second in righteousness, the third in
loving of Eternal Life. The first ends in '*Miserere mei Deus;*
have mercy on me O God'. The second in '*Misericordiam et
judicium cantabo tibi Domine;* Of mercy and judgement I will
sing to thee O lord'. The third at '*Laudate Dominum:* Praise
ye the Lord'. This book of all Holy Writ is the most used in
the services of Holy Church. Therefore in it is perfection of
divine writing, for it contains all that other books contain at
length. That is the law of the Old Testament and the New.
There is described the rewards of good men, the pains of

bad men, the discipline of penance, the growth of righteousness of life, the perfection of holy men who pass into
Heaven, the life of active men, the meditations of contem-
platives, and the love of contemplation, the highest that
may be in man living in the body, also what sin rives
(breaks) from man's soul, and what penance restores.

There is no need to tell everyone here, for through the
grace of God you shall find them set forth in their places.
This scripture is called the *Book of the Hymns of Christ.*
'Hymn' is loving of God with song. To one hymn falls
three things; love of God, joy of heart or thought and
yearning for God's love. Song is great happiness with
thoughts of everlasting things, and endless joy bursting
with the voice of love. Well is it called *The Book of Hymns*
for it teaches us to love God with good cheer and mirth,
pleasantness of soul, not only in heart, but also in voice,
loving and teaching those that are ignorant!

The mother of this book is Christ and his spouse, that is,
Holy Church, or every righteous man's soul. The intention
is to conform you that are besmirched in Adam, to Christ
in newness of life; sometimes the Psalm speaks of Christ in
his Godhead, sometimes in his manhood; sometimes he
uses the voice of his servants. Also he speaks of Holy
Church in three ways: Sometimes in the person of perfect
men, sometimes of imperfect men, sometimes of evil men
which are in Holy Church in body but not in soul, in name
not in deed, in number not in merit.

In this work I seek no strange English, but lightest and
commonest, and such as is most like Latin, so that they
who know no Latin, by the English may come to many
Latin words! In the translation I follow the letter as much
as I may and where I find no proper English, I follow the
sense of the word so that they who read it need not fear
any mistake. In expounding, I follow holy doctors, for it
may come into some envious man's hand who for something to say will assert that I don't know what I'm talking
about, and so do harm to himself and others if he despises
work that is profitable to himself and them.

Note: Miss E. H. Allen thinks that The Psalter was commenced about ten years before the enclosure of Richard's friend Dame Margaret Kirkby. She was enclosed at Anderby before she moved to Hampole after Richard's death in 1349. It will have taken some time to finish, while he was writing the *Incendium Amoris*, but before the three English Epistles. She says that the author of the 'Mirror of Our Lady', writing for the Nuns of Syon in the fifteenth century, refers to the accepted English text of the Psalms as those of 'Richard Rolle's drawing'.

From the English Psalter[17]

With Richard Rolle's Commentary on the Psalm

Psalm 13

Usque quo, Domine? 'How long forgetest thou me O Lord, to the end?'

'How long turnest thou thy face from me?' The voice of holy men that yearn for the coming of Jesus Christ, that they might live with him in joy, and complaining of delay, says 'Lord how long forgetest thou me, to the end?' 'That I long to have and hold.' That is, how long delayest thou me from the sight of Jesus Christ that is the right ending of my intention? And 'How long turnest thou thy face from me?' that is, when wilt thou give me perfect knowledge of thee? These words may none say truly, but a perfect man or woman has gathered together all the desires of their soul, and with the nail of love fastened them in Jesus Christ, so that they think an hour were too long to dwell away from him, for they long always for him. But they that love not have no longing that he may come, for their conscience tells them that they have not loved him as they should have done.

'How long must I seek counsels in my soul, with sorrow in my heart, daily?'

17. This translation is from *The Psalter or Psalms of David with a translation by Richard Rolle of Hampole*, edited by R. H. Bramley of Magdalen College, Oxford.

Yet the longing of a pure heart is eschewed. How long shall I take counsel in my heart of divers things? Great pain and suffering is seen here and woe: 'How long shall I be in adversity?' For man has no need of counsel but in adversity.

But I am in anguish and sorrow in my soul in the continual delay while my life lasts. For when we want a thing, and that thing is delayed the sorrow and yearning increases. And as no man lives here without temptation though he be never so perfect, he says 'How much longer must my enemy be exalted above me? Look, and hear me O Lord my God!' His Enemy he calls the Devil, or the ways of the flesh, that is exalted above him, and God suffers him to tempt him or torment him. But I am looking for help that I may be freed from this enemy. Hear me in this!

'Lighten my eyes that I may not any time sleep in death lest my enemy should say "I had the mastery over him".' Lighten with thy love the eyes of my heart, that I sleep not 'in death' that is that my eyes be not locked in the delight of sin. Then we sleep in death when the light of God's love is buried and quenched in us, and we have our delight in fleshly lust, or any other deadly sin lest mine enemy, that is the Devil, should say 'I had the mastery over him!' He makes his assault on us and boasts before God to make us be damned if he can overcome us in any temptation.

'They that anger me will be glad if I be stirred to wrath, but I hope in thy mercy.' The Devils that tempt us night and day, have none other joy, but to stir us up and make us fall into sin. They anger me to stir me to sin, and after stirring, watch when I fall, that they might crow over me!

'But I Lord hoped in thy mercy', and set nought by their stirring, no more than a giant does at the shoving of a weak man.

'My heart shall rejoice in thy salvation; I shall sing to our Lord for his goodness to me, and I shall sing in the name of the Lord in the Highest.' Thou shalt not only make me bright and burning in love for thee, also that mine enemy the Devil rejoice not, for if he be overcome, he shall be sorrowful! And my heart shall rejoice in thy Salvation that is in Jesus whom I behold in thought, and to him I shall sing in gladness of soul.

When all the powers of my soul are raised to the sound of Heaven, then may I sing with joy and resounding voice of that which belongs to the contemplative life, for his spirit is upon me. To sing to him in such longing! I shall sing with fervour to honour him! That belongs to the Active Life also to those who say 'I shall thank him joyfully in thought and deed!'

Of Three Workings in Man's Soul

A great clerk called Richard of St Victor[18] says in a book of contemplation, that in the soul of every Christian the mind works in three ways; thought, thinking, and contemplation. Thoughts that come into the head unbidden, demand no labour and bear no fruit. You can see this vain habit in every idle soul! Thinking demands labour, and bears fruit. Contemplation demands no labour, yet bears fruit.

You can see in your own soul that there is no need to steer your mind to entertain vain thoughts, for they will come all unsought. I think he said well that thought is without labour and fruit! Therefore for the love of God let not your life and soul be wasted by this vain habit, but leave this fruitless working in your soul, and pass on to that which bears fruit in spite of labour.

The more often that you work at it, the easier it will seem, and great abundance of sweetness if you will use it. Thinking with labour and fruit is when you make yourself think on anything with all your might, as of the Passion of Christ, your wretchedness, or the joys of the holy saints.

If you will labour at such thoughts, you shall find great fruit in them, and it shall be fruit of such sweetness beyond all telling, and then shall your labour be taken from you and you shall come to the third working, which is called contemplation.

Contemplation is without labour, but with great fruit. But my son, though you have great labour in meditation or thinking, this sweet gift of grace is not given to you but by the free gift of God. And wit you well, the more joy that you feel, the more you are bound to labour in prayer, and thinking, and loving God day and night.

If you will, I will show you a manner of thinking which is both prayer and thought; it is one of the joys of Our

---

[18.] The Victorine Canons, Paris. This Religious House produced notable scholars in the twelfth century, including Richard and Hugh of St Victor.

Lady, and how you shall think when you say your Hail
Mary, or else Our Lady's Psalter.

First you shall imagine in your soul a fair chamber, and
in that chamber you shall see Our Lady St Mary, sitting at
a window, and reading from a book. And you shall seat
yourself in some corner of that chamber, busily watching
her where she sits; her countenance, and her appearance.
See how demurely she sits, her book before her, reading
privately and silently.

There she read words of prophecy of Isaiah, that a
maiden should conceive and bear a Child which should
save all mankind. And she desired in her thought that she
might see that Blessed Lord that she had served in the
Temple in the form of man; attentively watch her, and you
shall see this imagination in her soul, looking in her book,
and then casting her eyes up to Heaven. Behold then the
blessed lovely face of that Lady, how devout she is, her
sweet mouth closed, and no breath nor sound passing out
of her mouth, and no redness in her face.

For my son, when a soul is fully ravished in the desire
of a thing all the blood is gathered into one place where
the soul most reigns, and that is in the heart. And the body
at that time seems dead, save a little warmth that lies in
the limbs and other parts of the body. But truly no one is
ravished to come to such joy, but those that spend their
days in devout prayers and meditation.

My son, two things I find Our Lady had in her soul. The
first was the *height* of desire, the second, the *ground* of
meekness. For these two she had ever, before the concep-
tion of Christ, and after. For without these two it is impos-
sible for any man to come to contemplation or the love of
God. For truly they be well knit together, meekness and
desire, for if they were parted asunder, then were they
both vices. For in desire without meekness hangs
presumption. And meekness without desire brings
despair, and when they be both together, they make a well
disposed soul.

And my son, keep well to these, and truly you shall

have your desire, and the Kingdom of Heaven to be your reward. How these two were in Our Lady's soul, I will tell you. I know well that from the time that she had read that Our Lord should take Man's nature, and be born of a maiden, she fell into such a longing for Our Lord, that she imagined the prophesy thus in her soul, saying these words in her mind.

'O Lord God, that it might be your blessed will that this thing might be in my time! What joy! What comfort! What bliss! What mirth! What reward might any soul have greater, than to see and serve that Blessed Lord being in our nature, so that both might be gladdened, our body in the service and sight of his body, and our soul in the love and fervour of his Godhead!'

And thus for the greatness of her longing, she said in her soul, these words of desire: 'O Lord, if it be thy dear will that I might be the handmaiden of that maiden that shall bear thy child!' And lo! Here the *height* of her desire, and here the *ground* of her meekness you well may see for she knew well that she was a maiden, and yet held herself so lowly and so unworthy that she desired not to be that same maiden, but with great love and dread, she prayed to be the handmaiden of that maiden, and wit you well that she thought herself unworthy of it.

Yet holding to the height of desire, and the ground of meekness, there appeared to her the Angel Gabriel in bodily form, kneeling beside her saying these words:

'Hail, full of Grace, the Lord is with thee!'

Thanks be to God.

Now my son, keep well these two things, and truly you shall have your desire, and the Kingdom of Heaven to be your reward. To which place may he bring us, who lives and reigns for ever and ever. Amen.

The Bee and the Ostrich

The bee has three characteristics. One is that she is never idle, and stays not with them that will not work, but casts them out and pushes them away. Another is that when she flies, she carries earth with her feet that she be not lightly blown too high by the wind. The third is that she keeps her wings clean and bright.

Thus righteous men that love God are never in idleness; for either they are working, praying, thinking or reading, or other good doings, or reproving idle men, and showing them they will not be worthy of the feast of Heaven if they will not work. Here they 'take earth' that is, they hold themselves humbly, that they be not blown away with the wind of vanity and pride!

They keep their wings clean, that is, the two commandments of Love they fulfil in good conscience; they have other virtues, unblemished with the filth of sin.

Aristotle says that the bees are fighting against him that would take their honey from them! So should we do against devils that would part us from the honey of pure life and grace, for many there are that never can keep the Commandments of Love towards friends, kinsmen or strangers, but either they love them over-much, if they favour them unjustly, or they love them too little if they do not as they should to them.

Such cannot fight for their honey, because the Devil turns it to wormwood and makes their souls bitter with anguish and restlessness and vain thoughts and other wretchedness, for they are so burdened by earthly friendship that they flee not to the love of Christ, in which they might well gather up the love of all creatures living on earth.

Wherefore accordingly, Aristotle says that some birds are good at flying and travel from one land to another, and some are bad at flying from heaviness of body, and their nest is not far from ground.

Thus it is with them that turn to God's service; some are

good at flying for they fly from earth to Heaven, and rest there in thought in the delight of God's love. Some there are that cannot fly from this earth, but seek love in one thing after another, and in various men and women as they come and go but in Jesus Christ they can find no sweetness; or if they any time feel anything it is too little to bring them to steadfastness, they are like a bird that is called ostrich that has wings but may not fly because of its weight. So they have understanding and fast and keep vigils and seem holy, but they cannot fly to love and contemplation of God, they are so full of other affections and other vanities.

Jesu in Truth

Jesu in truth there is no thing
In the wide world worth the winning,
To yearn for with love's longing
Save you beloved, my dear King!

Jesu, my love I owe to thee,
For me you died on the rood-tree.
Thy crown of thorns, thy nails three
The sharp spear that piercéd thee.

Jesu thy love is truth knowing,
Thy head bowed down, is love kissing,
Thine arms spread, is love embracing
Thy side all open, is love showing.

Jesu when I think of thee,
And look upon thy rood-tree
Thy sweet body bleeding I see,
Lord make that sight to wound me!

Close beside thee, by the Rood,
Then thy mother by thee stood,
Of love's tears she wept a flood,
For thy wounds and holy blood.

Jesu thou said'st 'All may see
That pass this way, here by me,
A while abide and come and see
If any in sorrow is like to me!'

Jesu is Love

Jesu is love that lasts alway,
For Him is our longing,
Jesu the night turns into day
The Winter into Spring.
Jesu think on us for ay,
For you we hold our King,
Give us grace as you well may,
To love you without ending.

Jesu now receive my heart,
And to your love me bring,
You are all of my desire,
I wait for your coming.
Then make me clean of deadly sin,
And let us never part,
And kindle me with fire within,
That your love I may win,
And hold you in my heart.

Jesu my soul pray mend,
Your love into me send:
That I with you may spend
Forever without end.
With love's sword wound my heart,
Raised up with you to be,
Dearly you have paid the fee,
Your true love I would be.

Love Longing

I sit and sing of love longing,
That in my breast is bred,
Jesu my king, my rejoicing,
When I were to thee led!

Sigh longingly both day and night,
For one so fair of hue!
There is no thing my heart may light,
But love that is aye new!

Who so had him in his sight,
Or in his heart him knew,
His darkest day turned joyful bright,
His sad heart happy grew!

In mirth he liveth night and day,
That loveth that sweet child,
It is Jesu in truth, I say,
Of all meekest and mild!

Wrath from him will all away,
Though he were ne'er so wild.
He that in heart loves him this day,
From evil he will him shield.

Mary Mother, Lady Bright

Mary mother, lady bright
Ever trusting in your might,
My heart's love, my life, my light,
Thou be my help both day and night!

Jesu, for love thou suffered wrong
Wounds sore and pains strong,
Thy rueful pains were full long
None may tell in word or song.

Jesu for love you suffered woe,
Streams of blood did from thee flow,
Thy sweet body was black and blue,
Our sins it made so, Well-a-woe!

Jesu thy crown, it sat full sore
They scourging when thou scourged were
It was for me, Jesu thy grace,
Thy pains, that you this suffering bore.

Jesu sweet, thou hanged on tree
Not for thy guilt, but all for me,
With my sin's guilt; so woe is me,
Sweet Jesu forgive it me!

Jesu when thou strainéd were
Thy pains were more and more,
Mary ay with thee was there
With sorrowful cheer and sighing sore.

Jesu why were you painéd so
That never did'st wrong nor woe?
It was for me and many more
That thou so hardly were done to.

Jesu for love

Jesu for love thou hanged on rood,
For love thou gavest thy heart's blood,
Love you made our soul's food,
Thy love brought us to good.

Jesu my true love, thou madest free
For all thou did'st for love of me.
What for that shall I yield thee?
Thou askest nought but love, of me!

Jesu my dear, my love, my light,
I will thee love, that is but right!
Make me love thee with all my might,
And for thee yearn both day and night.

Jesu make me so love thee
That ever my thoughts upon thee be,
With thy sweet eyes you look on me,
And mildly my doings see.

Jesu thy love be all my thought.
Of other things I reckon nought,
But that my love to thee be brought
And thou hast me so dearly brought!

Jesu though I sinful be,
Full long hast thou spared me,
So more ought I to love thee,
That thou to me hast been so free.

Mary mild, gentle, kind,
Pray for me, thou hear'st my call:
When my soul is gone from me,
That I may your dear son see!

Jesu Thou be all my Yearning!

Jesu, beauty ask I not,
Nor proud clothes, nobly wrought,
Brooches, nor rings dearly bought,
But heart's love, and clean thought.

Jesu when it liketh thee,
Love's sparkles send thou me!
Make my heart warm to thee,
Burning in the love of thee!

Jesu thy mercy comforteth me,
For none may so sinful be,
But sin will leave and from thee flee,
That he may mercy find in thee.

Jesu though I sinful be,
I have ever trust in thee
Dear Lord, I pray thee
That of my sins thou do mend me.

Jesu grant that I may see
The great goodness thou hast done for me,
And I unkind against thee!
Forgive me Lord that art so free.

Jesu if thou from me go,
My heart is full of sorrow and woe,
That thou art gone me fro'.
What may I do but cry 'O Woe!'.

Jesu my love, teach thou me,
With all my heart to love thee,
With thy might make it so be
And thereto Lord, constrain thou me.

Jesu my Life, my Lord, my King.
For thee my soul hath great longing,
Thou hast it wedded with thy ring,
When thy will is, to thee it bring.

Jesu that dearly boughtest me
Make me worthy to come to thee
All my sins forgive thou me,
That I may come and dwell with thee!

Jesu fair, my lover bright,
I pray thee with heart and might
Bring my soul into thy light,
Where it is day and never night.

Jesu, thy help at my ending!
Take my soul at my dying,
Send it succour and comforting
That it dread no wicked thing.

Jesu, Jesu, blessed is he,
That in thy joy, thee shall see,
And have fully the love of thee,
Sweet Jesu, grant it me!

Jesu thy bliss hath no ending,
There is no sorrow or greeting, (crying)
But pity and joy with great liking,
Sweet Jesu, thereto us bring!

Sweet Jesu, Now Will I Sing

Sweet Jesu, now will I sing,
To thee a song of love-longing.
Make in my heart a well-spring,
Thee to love over everything!

Sweet Jesu king of bliss,
My heart's love, my heart's lisse! [comfort]
In love Lord thou me wisse, [know]
Let me never thy love miss!

Sweet Jesu my heart's light,
Thou art day without the night
Give me both grace and might
For to love thee aright!

Sweet Jesu, my soul's boot, [remedy]
In my heart thou set a root
Of thy love that is so sweet,
And it tend, that it may shoot!

Unkind Man

Unkind man, give heed to me,
And look what pain I suffer for thee!
Sinful man on thee I cry,
As only for thy love I die
Behold the blood from me down runs,
Not for my guilt, but for thy sins
My hands my feet with nails are fast,
Sinews and veins are wrenched at last.
The blood runs out at my heart beat,
Look it falls down to my feet!
Of all the pains I suffer sore,
Within my heart it grieves me more
The unkindness that I find in thee,
That for thy love thus hanged on tree.
Alas, why loves thou me not
And I thy love so dear has bought?
But thou my love thou does me wrong,
Since I have loved thee long.
Two and thirty year and more
I was for thee in travail sore,
With hunger, thirst, heat and cold
For thy love bought and sold,
Pained, nailed and done on tree,
All man, for the love of thee.
Love thou me as thou well may,
And from thy sin draw thee away.
I give thee my body with wounds sore,
And thereto shall I give thee more:
Over all this I-wisse
In earth my grace, in Heaven my blisse.
Amen.

The Lay Folk's Mass Book
(Abridged)

Introduction

The Mass, the central act of worship in the Church, is a solemn renewal and participation in time through the Holy Eucharist in the eternal work of salvation, the Incarnation of the divine person of Jesus Christ as perfect man and his sacrifice on the Cross, and Resurrection.

The Fathers of the Seventh Ecumenical Council say: 'He (God) recreated him (man) into immortality by giving him this invaluable gift. This re-creation was more in God's image and likeness than the first creation – this gift is eternal'. Of the communion with the divine beauty and glory it is said: 'God became man that man may become God.'[19]

The High Mass on a Sunday with the procession of the clergy, the celebrant, deacon, subdeacon, acolytes, cross-bearer, candles, banners, thurifers, the asperges, music, and the activity behind the rood screen which separated the sanctuary from the nave, may appear today to have been a distancing of the clergy from the people who, without stools, knelt or stood or perhaps moved about. This was in contrast to the low Masses on weekdays at side altars or in tiny chantry chapels held for sick relatives, for the dead, or for various other of the people's intentions.

---

[19] This phrase is originally from Irenaeus, and subsequently became central to all eastern soteriology.

Holy Communion was less frequently received by the laity in the Middle Ages, but the Easter Communion was universal and the death-bed 'Housel'[20] devoutly prayed for. Many people would attend Mass daily 'to see their Maker' and adore, and those at home or in the fields would worship at the sound of the Sacring Bell and the Angelus. As people of all classes participated in the building, maintenance and the liturgical activities of the church, so it was to them a focal point, a community centre, and as it would be said today, their 'Expressive Arts Centre'.

While the learned followed the Latin of the Mass, others would have read the prayers in English, and the illiterate would have said '*Paters and Aves*', the Rosary, or their own prayers. The thinking behind the low Mass was not to disturb the prayers of the faithful, who, watching the priest at the altar, would have recognised the signs of when to stand and to kneel. Though the laity received Holy Communion less frequently, they participated in the *Pax*, a ritual corresponding to the Kiss of Peace. From apostolic times, the Kiss of Peace had been exchanged, but by modern times prior to Vatican II it had become enacted only by the clergy. In the Middle Ages, the priest kissed the *Pax-brede*, a disk of gold or silver engraved with a representation of the Crucifixion, and this was passed to all the congregation to kiss. At the end of Mass, a loaf provided by a parishioner in turn, was cut up and distributed. This 'Wayfaring Bread' could be eaten or taken home and is a custom still followed in the East.

Richard Rolle is thought to have translated this Mass Book from Norman French, the work of Dan Jeremy, because of the prayer at the Elevation, 'Loved be thou King' which is known to be by Rolle who has turned it into English Rhyming couplets and begins:

'Dan Jeremy says'.

---

[20] Holy Communion, the consecrated wafer, the Host, given to the dying as part of the Last Rites, the Viaticum ('provision for the journey').

The Preparation

'Thou at Mass good attention take,
That thou at Mass no chattering make.

When the priest speaks, or if he sing,
To him thou give good harkening.'

Therefore kneeling on thy knees
Each beside the other, says

'Shrive thee there of all thy sins,
Beginning thus when he begins

All Next beneath this rubric stands
And there – with jointly hold thy hands.'

Confiteor

Many saying Confiteor, were good all saying this therefore.

I acknowledge to God, full of might
And to his Mother, Maiden bright,

And to all Hallows here
And to the Father Ghostly,

That I have sinned greatly
In many sins black,

In thought and speech and in delight,
In word and work, I am to blame;

Therefore I pray that in God's name,
St Mary and all Hallows holy

And the priest, to pray for me,
That God have mercy and pity.

And give me grace and forgiveness
For my misdeeds.

So then, standing, I would that thou wert saying this:

> God, for thy goodness,
> At the beginning of this Mass,
>
> Grant all that it shall hear
> In conscience be clean and clear.
>
> Lord save the priest that it shall say,
> From temptations all today.
>
> That he be clean in deed and thought,
> That evil spirits annoy him not.
>
> That he fulfil this sacrament
> With pure heart and good intent.
>
> Forst wholly to thine honour,
> That sovereign is of all succour,
>
> And to thy Mother, maiden pure
> And to all that hear it soul's health.
> Health and grace, and kindred's health,
>
> And rest and peace that lasts ay,
> To Christian souls passed away.
>
> And to us all thy succour send,
> And bring us to joy without an end.

Gloria in Excelsis

On high feast or on Holy days, when one either sings or says Gloria in Excelsis in the Mass, say all that herein written is.

Joy be unto God in Heaven, and all kinds of mirth that men may know, and peace on earth to all righteous men of good will.

We love thee Lord God Almighty, and we bless thee, we
worship thee, thou all-worthy art, and increasest our joy!
We thank thee Lord of all grace for thy great joy that thou
hast. Our Lord our God, our Heavenly King, Our God our
Father Almighty: Our Lord the Son of God of Heaven,
Jesus Christ, comely to Know! Our Lord, Lamb of God we
name thee, Son of God the Gracious Father, thou hast
withered the world's sin, have mercy on us for great and
small!

> Thou hast wasted the world's wrack!
> Our praise in this time take!
>
> Thou sittest on the Father's right hand,
> With Mercy help us in this land!
>
> For thou art holy, only of thyself Lord, thou alone,
>
> Thou art highest of wisdom most,
> Jesus Christ with the Holy Ghost,
>
> And with the Father of Heaven,
>
> In more joy than man may know,
> To that joy Jesus us show!
>
> Though the prayer of the Mother. Amen.

And when thou hast all this done,
Kneel down on thy knees soon.
If they sing Mass or if they say,
Thy Pater Noster rehearse alway.

The deacon or priest the Gospel reads.
Stand up then and take good heed.

The Gospel

For then the priest flits his book
North to that other altar nook,

And makes a cross upon the letter
With his thumb he speeds the better

And then another upon his face
For he has much need of grace;

For then an earthly man shall know,
The words of Jesus Christ, God's son of Heaven!

Stand and say in this manner, All thou mayst see written here:

In the name of the Father, Son and the Holy Ghost

O True God of most might,
Be God's word welcome to me,
Joy and living Lord, be to thee.

Whilst it is read, speak thou not,
But think on him that dear thee bought

Saying all this in thy mind,
All that shalt after written find:

Jesu my Love, grant me thy grace,
And amendment time and space.

The good to choose, and leave the ill.

And that it so may be
Good Jesu grant it me! Amen.

Men are to say the Creed sometime,
When they say theirs, look thou say thine.

This that follows in English letter,
Would that thou say it for the better.

What they say here, say thou, none else,
But do forth all this book tells.

Hereto, look thou take good heed!
For here is written thine English Creed!

Credo

I believe in God, Father of might,
That all has wrought, Heaven and earth,
Day and night, and all of nought.
And in Jesu, God's only son,
That was so mild
Both God and Man, lord endless
In him I believe,
Though making of the Holy Ghost,
He lay in Mary, maiden chaste
That was so mild,
Became a child!
Under Pontius Pilate scourged he was,
Us for to save,
Done on the cross and dead he was,
And laid in a grave;
The soul of him went into Hell,
Though truth to say,
Up he rose in flesh and felle [skin]
On the third day;
He leapt to Heaven,
And sittest on his father's right side
In majesty;
Thence he shall come, us all to deem, [judge]
In his manhood
Quick and dead, all that has been
Of Adam's seed
Well I believe in the Holy Ghost.
And Holy Church that is so good;
And so I believe that Housel is
Both flesh and blood;

And of my sins forgiveness if I will mend,
Uprising also of my flesh and life without end.

Offertory

After that, fast at hand
Comes the time of offering.

Offer or leave, whether thou list. [please]
How thou should'st pray, I would thou wist. [knew]

Whiles thou standest I rede thou say. [*rede* – advise]
All next is written, God to pay:

> Jesu that was in Bethl'em born,
> And three Kings came thee before,
>
> They offered gold, incense and myrrh,
> And thou forsook none of these
>
> But wished them well all three
> Home again in their country.
>
> Right so our offerings we offer,
> And our prayers that we proffer
>
> And take Lord for thy loving,
> And be our help in everything,
>
> That all perils be undone,
> Our good desires grant us soon.
>
> Of our misdeeds, thou us amend,
> In all our need succour send. Amen

Say Pater Noster, get upstanding.
All the time the priest is washing

Till after washing, the priest will salute
The altar and then turn about.

Then he asks with still steven [quiet voice]
Every man's prayers to God in Heaven

Take good notice of the priest
When he turns, Knock on thy breast,

And think then for thy sin,
Thou art not worthy to pray for him

But when thou pray'st, God sees thy will,
If it be good, forgets thine ill

Therefore with hope in his mercy
Answer the priest with this in view.

Secret

Then the priest goes to his book
His Private prayers for to look

Then he begins 'Per Omnia'
And after 'Sursum Corda'

At the end say 'Sanctus' thrice
'in Excelsis' he says twice,

As fast as ever he has done,
Look that thou be ready soon,

And say these words with still steven [quiet voice]
Privily to God in Heaven.

> In world of words, without ending,
> Thanked be Jesu my King!
>
> All my heart I give it thee,
> Great right it is that so it be.
>
> With all my will I worship thee!
> Jesu blessed may thou be.

With all my heart I thank it thee,
The good that thou hast done to me.

Sweet Jesu, grant me now this,
That I may come unto thy bliss!

There with angels for to sing
This sweet song of thy loving:

Sanctus, Sanctus Sanctus,
Jesu grant that it be thus. Amen

Canon

When this is said, Kneel thou down,
And that with good devotion

For all thy good, thank God then
And pray also for every man.

For every state, and each degree
So wills the law of charity.

Therefore without tarrying,
In this wise be thy saying:

Lord honoured may thou be
With all my heart I worship thee

I Thank thee for all I owe,
Of more good than I can know!
I thank thee Lord, I pray also

That all my guilt thou me forgive
And be my help while I shall live,

And give me grace for to eschew
To do that thing that me should rue.

And give me will ay well to work.
Lord think on the state of Holy Kirk,

The Pope and bishops, priests, and clerks;
That they be kept in all good works.

The King, the Queen, the Lords of the land that they be well maintaining their states in all goodness, and rule the folk in righteousness.

Our kinsmen and our well-wishers, our friends, tenants and servants, old men, children and all women, merchants, craftsmen and tillers, I pray the lord for them all, that they be kept specially in good health, and live holily.

To them that are in illness lying, slandered, in discomfort, or constrained,

Sick or in prison or upon the sea
Poor, exiled, deserted, if there be

To all of them thou send succour,
To thy worship and thine honour.

To all that are in good life today
Keep them Lord from all folly
And from all sin for thy mercy,

And give them grace to last and lend
In thy service to their end.

This world that turns many ways,
God turn to us in all our days

The fruits of the earth make plenteous,
All thou seest best ordain for us,

And such grace to us thou send,
That in our last day, at our end,

When this world and we shall sever,
Bring us to joy that lasts forever! Amen.

Elevation

Look Pater Noster thou be saying,
When the chalice he be signing [with the Cross]

Then the time is near of sacring, [consecration]
A little bell men use to ring:

Then shall thou do reverence
To Jesu Christ's own presence,

That may loose all baleful bands,
Kneeling hold up both thy hands
And so the Elevation thou behold.

Therefore I rede with good intent,
That thou behold this sacrament

Such prayers then thou make,
As likes thee best to take.

Short prayers should be without dread
And therewith Pater Noster and the Creed.

If thou of one be unprepared
I set here one that may be said,

Though I mark it here in letter
Thou may'st change it for a better!

Lord be thou King
And thanked be thou King

And blessed be thou King
Jesu all my joying!

Of all thy gifts good
That for me spilt thy blood
And died upon the rood.

Thou give me grace to sing
The song of thy loving.

Thy mercy Jesu would I have
And for fearing durst it not crave,

But thou bids ask, and we shall have
Sweet Jesu, thou me save,

And give me wit and wisdom right
To love thee Lord with all my might!

Lord by thy holy grace,
Hear our prayers in this place!

Grant O Lord, for our prayer,
That Christian souls that pass from here,

That from this life that sinful is
That each one share in this Mass;

For their souls should I pray dearly
That I may know truly,

That this Mass may be their meed! [reward]
Help and health from all kinds dread:

Father's soul, Mother's soul, brother dear,
Sister's soul, Kinsmen, and folk sincere

That us good would, or us good did
And to all that in Purgatory pine,
This Mass be meed and medicine.

To all Christian souls duly,
Grant thy grace and thy mercy;

Forgive them all of their trespass,
Loose their bonds and let them pass

From all pain and from all care
To joy that lasts for evermore. Amen.

Pater Noster

Look Pater Noster thou be praying,
Until thou hear the priest be saying

'per omnia saecula' [on height]
Then I would thou stand upright

For he will say with high steven [loud voice]
Pater Noster to God in Heaven.

Harken to him with good will
And while he says it hold thou still

But answer at 'Temptationem'
Sed libera nos a malo. Amen

It were no need for this to ken, [know]
For who ken not this are unlearned men.

Father, ours that is in Heaven,
Blessed be thy name to know,

Come to us thy Kingdom!
In Heaven and earth thy will be done,

Our each day bread grant us today
And our misdeeds forgive us ay,

As we do them that trespass us,
Right so have mercy upon us,

Lead us to no foundering
But shield us from each wicked thing. Amen.

Agnus Dei

He says Agnus, thrice ere he cease,
The last word, he speaks of peace.

In that peace thou may not be
If thou be out of charity.

Then is good, of God to crave
That thou charity may have.

There when the priest Pax will kiss [sign of peace]
Kneel thou and pray then this:

> God's lamb that best may
> Do the sin of this world away,
>
> On us have mercy and pity,
> And grant us peace and charity,
>
> For in Charity are three kinds of love
> That for perfect peace indeed behoves.
>
> The first love is certainly
> To love the Lord sovereignly.
>
> Therefore I pray thee God of Might
> Thou make me love both day and night
>
> As to my sovereign, thee to pay,
> In all that ever I can or may.
>
> And pressed be I early and late
> To my degree and mine estate.
>
> All good deeds to fulfil
> And to eschew all that are ill.
>
> The second is a private love,
> That is needful in my behoof,

Which love is properly
Betwixt my soul and body,

Therefore make me, good Lord,
My body and soul of one accord,

That either part by one assent,
Serve thee with good intent.

Let never my body do that ill
That it may my soul spill!

The third love is, without doubt,
To love each neighbour me about,

And of that love for nothing cease.
Therefore I pray thee Prince of Peace,

That thou wilt make as thou may'st best
Me to be in peace and rest.

And ready to love all manner of men
My kinsfolk namely, then

Neighbours, servants and each sugete, [retainer]
Fellows friends, none to forget,

But love each one far or near,
As myself with heart clear.

And by virtue of this Mass
We might have forgiveness

Of all our guilt, and all our miss,
And by thy help come to thy bliss!

Post Communion

When the priest has rinsing done,
Upon thy feet thou stand up soon.

Then the clerk flits the book
Again to the south altar nook,

Then without tarrying
In this wise be thou saying;

Jesu my King I pray to thee,
Bow down thine eyes of pity

And hear my prayer in this place,
Lord God by thy holy grace,

For me and all that here are
That thou wilt keep us from every woe,

That may befall in any way
In our deeds we do today.

We pray this Mass may stand instead
Of shrift, and also housel-bread.
          [Confession and Communion]

And Jesu by thy wounds five
Show us the way of righteous life. Amen.

When this is said, kneel down soon
Say Pater Noster till Mass be done.

For the Mass has not ceased
Before the 'Ite missa est'

When thou hears said 'Ite'
Or 'Benedicamus' if it be.

Then is the Mass all done
But yet this prayer make thou right soon,

After it well thou may
In God's name wend thy way.

In mind of God I me bless,
With thy blessing God, send me hence.

Blessing

In Nomine Patris et Filii, et Spiritus Sancti, Amen.

How thou at Mass thy time should spend,
Have I told, now will I end!

The Office of St Richard, Hermit

(From The Office of St Richard for after he will have been canonised by the Church.)

In the meantime, neither the Canonical Hours, nor the Solemnisation is licenced to be sung in the church. With the evidence of his undoubted holiness, it is permitted to venerate him, and seek his intercession in private prayers.[21]

AT VESPERS

Antiphon   Rejoice Holy Mother Church! Let praises resound, Rejoice happy fatherland England, which St Richard has endowed with glory!

Psalms of the Day

Antiphon   St Richard, taught by the Spirit, lived a life of prudent renounciation, that he might gain a more excellent dwelling hereafter.

Antiphon   With starry rapture, with burning love, he prays frequently to follow the saints and live in grace.

[21.] This is a translation from the York Breviary, Surtees Soc., Vol. II app. V, 1882.

Antiphon   He cures the sick and the deaf and the dumb
             and the afflicted.
             (Psalm XLIII/42. Like as the Hart desireth the
             Water Brooks etc)

Versicle   He shows forth love.

Response   The love of the Beloved One.

Office Hymn

On the feast of Richard pray
To follow in his steps today
We loudly sing, we're in his debt
His triumph is our benefit

The fire of love it warmed his heart,
He felt and suffered love's sharp dart.
This holy one with love grew pale,
But trusted love would soon prevail.

With sweetest fruit of blessed bees,
So his honied speech agrees,
As honey from the comb expressed
His teaching is the sweetest, best.

He is enwrapt, seraphic mortal,
Borne to Heaven's starry portal.
Praying with absorbed devotion
Raising hands in adoration.

O Triune God, your children pray,
Our souls make true and pure today,
So rooted in your love we may
United be with you for ay!

Versicle   I have longed to sit beneath his shade,

Response   And his fruit is sweet in my mouth.

Antiphon   Oh how they extol thee with tales of love,
            Thy writings which inspire to holiness,
            wonderful preaching and powerful example,
            and pleasant manners.

Magnificat

My soul magnifies the Lord:
My spirit hath rejoiced in God my Saviour.
For he hath regarded the humility of his hand-maiden,
For behold from henceforth, all generations shall call me
    blessed.
For he that is mightly hath done great things to me: and
    holy is his name.
And his mercy is on all that fear him from generation to
    generation.
He hath showed the strength of his arm: he hath scattered
    the proud in the conceit of their heart.
He hath put down the mightly from their seat; and hath
    exalted the humble.
He hath filled the hungry with good things: and the rich
    he hath sent away empty.
He hath received his servant Israel, being mindful of his
    mercy.
As he spoke to our fathers: to Abraham and his seed forever.
Glory be to the Father, and to the son, and to the Holy Ghost.
As it was in the beginning is now and ever shall be, world
    without end amen.

Concluding Prayer

O God who by the example of the most holy Richard,
taught us to despise the things of earth, and with sincere
hearts aspire to the things of Heaven, grant that we may
by his merits and help, imitate the same and come to share
thy blessed delights for ever, through Jesus Christ Our
Lord, Amen.

Select Bibliography

Allen, H. E., *English Writings of Richard Rolle* (Oxford University Press, 1931).

Allen, H. E., *Writings Ascribed to Richard Rolle* (New York, D. C. Heath and Co., 1927).

Bramley, R. H., *The Psalter or Psalms of David with a translation by Richard Rolle of Hampole* (Clarendon Press, 1884).

Comper, F. M. M. (tr.), *Life and Lyrics of Richard Rolle* (London, 1928). The lyrics are in modern English and Rolle's life is sympathetically portrayed.

Horstmann, Carl (ed.), *Yorkshire Writers: Richard Rolle of Hampole and his Followers* (London, Swannn Sonnenschein, 1895). A valuable collection of Latin and Middle English works.

Surtees Society, *The York Breviary* (Vol. 75, Appendix 75, 1882). Source of biographical details and unascribed quotations.

Wolters, Clifton (tr.), *The Fire of Love* (London, Penguin, 1972). Translated from Latin into modern English with a very good introduction to Rolle.

Index

Printed in the United Kingdom
by Lightning Source UK Ltd.
130458UK00001B/220-402/P

9 780852 441237